CONTENTS

.

Spark A Dream

Poems and Encouragement Delivered By

Ebony Rose

ROSES FOR YOU

The saying is, "Give people their flowers while they yet Live".   I pray the words of this book blossom to honor the people in my life that mean so much to me. Mama we made it! Your unwavering confidence in my abilities pushes me daily. Stephanie and Raven, the love I have for you ladies is a rose in constant bloom. Winter Jade, you are the greatest gift I've received. My gift back to you is the message in this book. You are designed and equipped to fulfill whatever your heart desires. Auntie loves you 10!!!!!!!!!!!!!!!!!!!

ACKNOWLEDGMENTS

In the words of my great friend Tree, 'team work makes the dream work'. Thank you to EVERYONE that lent a listening ear, a helping hand, or an encouraging word. I couldn't have done it without you. A special thank you to Tiffany 'The Wordmatician' Scales for offering her editing expertise. Krystle Cesar, I asked for a cover that reflects the content of the book and still takes my breathe away. You DELIVERED. Carlos Wallace thank you for the gems of wisdom and priceless advice on being a successful author it Is helping me tremendously.

PURPOSE

How many people do you think have existed since the beginning of time?

As of April 2017, the world's population is estimated at 7.5 billion, (yes BILLION!!), 7,500,000,000 people venturing about the Earth. I can only imagine the sextillions of souls that have and continue to journey into the land of the living. The thing that amazes me the most, is out of all the people that have existed; no two people have possessed the same fingerprint. NOT EVEN IDENTICAL TWINS!!!

The overused term 'unique' has been chewed into a lackluster cliché. Its flavor is rejuvenated by the fact that there's really only **ONE** YOU!!! No one like you has ever existed, and no one like you ever will.

'ONE YOU!'

There is a reason why YOU are alive right now, at this very moment. Intertwined in the happenings of this generation and not captured in still black and whites or the future awaiting the arrival of your brilliance . There is something inside of YOU that is needed NOW!!

This generation's ears are ripe for the harvest of words YOU have to say, their eyes hungry for the visuals you cook up, hearts and souls thirsty for what exists in your well. The social climate is just right for the creative storm YOU are. The idea YOU are ~~afraid~~ to present, the dream you are hesitant to pursue, is exactly what this world needs, NOW.

YOU transitioned into this time for a purpose. Everyone has a purpose! Everything that was created by the creator has a divine purpose. The sun, water, ants...even manure. Come on!!! If manure has a specific purpose, why not YOU?

pur·pose

/ˈpərpəs/

noun: **purpose**; plural noun: **purposes**

1.the reason for which something is done or **created** or for which something exists.

The first order of business is to identify your purpose. Your purpose is designed to be a compass and a filter. It will guide YOU through inexorable obstacles and daunting decisions. The knowledge of your purpose will

purify distractions and negativity from your life.

PAUSE.

BREATHE.

Think about love.

Think about what you love.

Think about what you love to do.

Love, in this context is defined as fulFILLing,

enJOYable, satisfying, and completing. These words

are not typically related to the chest caving

compressions felt when charged with the task of

4

'finding your purpose'. The beautiful thing is life has been preparing YOU for your purpose all along. It might be writing, making others laugh, dancing, cooking, etc. What subjects do others turn to you for advice? Work out regimens? Budgeting tips? The possibilities are endless.

Celebrate the fact that discovering your purpose is NOT an impossible task. When you discover your purpose (it is GOING to happen), YOU are slapped, jabbed, and pummeled by the clarity of your eureka moment you will finally see your life clearly. I will never forget the day the landscape of my life became free of distracting debris. It was a humid Monday night, I was fortunate to make it to my church's prayer meeting. I distinctively remember making the conscious decision to submit completely to Yahweh.

Yah·weh

/ˈyäˌwā/

noun

1. a form of the Hebrew name of God used in the Bible. The name came to be regarded by Jews (c.300 BC) as too sacred to be spoken, and the vowel sounds are uncertain.

     I left my sins in the carpet and my burdens in the air. My open hands joined a prayer circle with my mom, aunt, and a gentleman I had NEVER seen a day before in my life.

     This moment, my pastor and I were spiritually in sync. As my petitions took flight to land at God's throne, those same petitions departed from his lips.

     Gifts. Purpose. Gifts. Purpose.

The center of my chest was the stage for the great blossoming of awakening. Literally, it felt like something was opening in the center of my chest. My third eye friends will say this was my Anahata (heart) chakra healing. Logic points back to love. It is said that the heart chakra bridges earthly and spiritual aspirations. I accept this to be fact.

That muggy Monday night, my mortal vessel was the host of the phenomenon of Heaven manifesting on Earth. I boarded the plane of purpose at the intersection of Divine and Timing. The aforementioned unknown gentleman located me after Amen and blessed me with a message.

"God told me to tell you, you are going to write a book of poetry and that is going to be your way to minister to people"

I felt like I could breathe for the first time.

PAUSE.

BREATHE.

<u>PROMISE</u>

I was told, you can't trap air.. .

Not even

for that one moment

you're struggling...on your last breathe

yearning to utter one last 'I love you'

It's a free spirit, it slips through the slits of your tightest

fist, roaming free on the other side

Whispering secrets to the spring leaves and in winter

finding nowhere to hide

To know this air face-to-face

might be a greatness that never graces our mundane

eyelids

But we feel you in a real way

In your presence, we jump out of our skin

Excited flesh rise forming braille so you can read us

We know for a fact you're real

You can be as gentle as a baaaahing of a lamb

Christmas morning in the dust of Bethlehem

Or as violent as raging lovers burning with betrayal

I ask myself how we can appreciate the nectar of life

without holding it

Just letting it visit our lungs for round trips

With no stops or souvenirs, no hellos or goodbyes

I needed something that felt at home in my hands

A wind heavy with the weight of fulfillment

So God blew a promise my way

His exhale gut punched my expectations

Knocked the wind right out of me, made me realize I

wasn't breathing on my own

It rattled my reality, blew my wind chime mind, sent

chills with conviction

Finally, there was a wind that would anchor me, as I

ride the moody tides of life

This wind set my sails for the promise land

Who knows the wilderness doesn't feel like the

wilderness when there's a promise in your hand?

Traveling fearlessly through jungles and ill lit valleys

armed and armored with air

That came in handy when my dreams were struggling

on their last breath

On the eve of farewell

I remembered the promise is filled with life down to the

very atom, ask Adam

My soul gets all gymnast when the air visits

Displaying portraits and glimpses of what's to come

It whispers secrets to my future

When my doubts form damns and stop my flow...there

the promise go

When I'm against so many odds it looks like I'll never

break even...there the promise go

When my compass won't guide me, when my feet land

in quick sand...there the promise go

Don't act for one second that this isn't the wind from

the 2nd chapter of acts, that will cause you to act in

split seconds.

I never knew air would be a sturdy foundation to stand on

Making the bad times, feel like good times keeping my head above water

J.J, Jehovah Jireh, making away when no one else could... Was dynamite

I tried to make to make my plans work, but they were temporarily laid off

Thank the heir for the breath of promise, allowing me to have it in my mind before it was in my hands

"Definiteness of purpose is the starting

point of all achievement."

+ W. Clement Stone

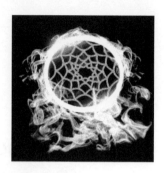

Igniting Moment

What does the W. Clement Stone quote above make

you feel?

<u>GIFTED</u>

The reality is you would not be given a purpose without the means to bring it from thought to reality. Yahweh/God/The higher power/The Universe wouldn't torture you like that. God's omnipotent-self, knew you would NEED your gift. When you decided to look for it, he wanted it to be easy to find. He put it where it was impossible for you to lose or .... It. So, he put it inside of you! That is why so many things are designed to make you lose yourself. Did you know are gifted? Right now, declare, I am gifted.

I am gifted.

I am gifted.

I am gifted.

[Look in the mirror]

I am gifted.

I am gifted.

Play this tune on repeat, until the record is broken and YOU BELIEVE it!

You have a gift, even if it is not as obvious as an American Idol winning singing voice or a Picasso brush stroke. You could have an eye for design, problem solving, or programming. Whatever it is that you do, it comes as easily as breathing and it makes you FEEL alive. So easily you mistakenly undervalue it...you don't deem it a talent or a gift at all. People might even come to you on countless occasions for advice on the topic.

Guess what?

That makes you an expert!

Can the sign be any louder? Your gift is the vehicle that gets you to your destined purpose, if you have the drive. Belief is the key that gets your car going and motivation is the fuel.

Guess what, your gift has been with you, your ENTIRE life! 90% of the experience that you've gained occurred when you were totally unaware. Why? It comes naturally. You are able to operate in the arena of your gift without too much effort, and the effort you exude is enjoyable.

My favorite example of natural inclination being the key to success is Steve Harvey. As a child Steve was a comedian before he even knew the occupation existed. Steve would tell jokes with his dad amidst the smoke of the bar-b-que pit, self-proclaimed comical church commentator, and of course class clown. He had a natural affection for making people laugh! Comedy catapulted Steve into the entertainment mogul that we know today.

How did he know?

What made him pursue his passion?

Steve was caught in the monotonous cycle of clocking in, clocking out, clocking in, clocking out to a desk job he dreaded. One night he decided to break his routine and entered into a comedy competition. Steve left the battle of laughs with trophy in hand. The shiny symbol of victory was Steve's cue to pursue comedy full-time.

What do you think Steve did on that mundane Monday morning?

Steve skipped into work and packed up his desk with a smile on his face. His bossed told him to pause his plan and think his new bride and their new born twins. This reminder of responsibility prompted Steve to politely go back to his desk and redecorate. As he's making his cubicle feel like home, a stranger randomly walks up and tells Steve he is the funniest guy he's every met. Steve proceeded to leave his security blanket and uncover the journey that led him to today.

As you embark on the journey to fulfilling/discovering your gift there are a few questions you must expose your mind to.

What activity makes you feel alive?

_____

_____

_____

What will you do when you get your ah-ha moment?

_____

_____

_____

_____

_____

_____

_____

_____

_____

_____

_____

_____

I am already celebrating with you! This is a step that can't be skipped. It's your navigation for all things going forward.

'The meaning of life is to find your gift.

The purpose of life is to give it away.'

+Pablo Picasso

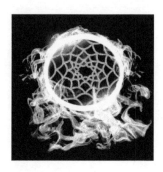

<u>Igniting Moment</u>

What does the Pablo Picasso quote above mean to

you?

__Unwrapped__

What is a gift that is unwrapped?

But merely a decorated intention

Intended to put an indention on

mediocrity

Purpose paused by pretty paper

Incarcerated by fear and practicality

The life line to flat lining hope

Breath of fresh air to gasping lungs

Water for chocolate Wasted.

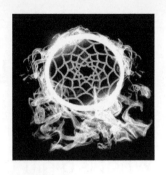

Igniting Moment

Soon as I accepted my calling and began using my gift of poetry to magnify God and encourage others, ALL types of doors opened to me! I performed at the Super Bowl in Houston and was featured works that would later be published in this very book. I went from forgetting lines at my first slam in 2014 to being on a Top Five Nationally Ranked Slam Poetry Team in 2017.

"A man's gift makes room for him and brings him before great men'

+ Proverbs 18:16

Pro Tip: Place your name in the scripture to see it manifest in your life. Ex: 'Ebony's gift makes room for her and brings her before great people'

THE C-WORD

In the game of dream fulfillment Rule number 1, remove 'Can't' from your vocabulary. The only thing you can accomplish with the forbidden C-word operating in your atmosphere is...nothing. The C-word produces excuses for why you aren't producing. The only thing a fruitless tree is good for, is casting shade. (you'll catch that one later). One movie that is a cultural staple holding us together is Love and Basketball. One of my favorite scenes is when young Quincy couldn't master a task, and his father heard him say, 'I can't do this sh##'. His dad was more offended by his son saying 'can't' than by his profanity. He expressed his son the importance of removing the c-word from his vocabulary.

The C-word is a demotivating, immobilizing,

settling, dream killing disease.

If you really are ready to succeed eliminate the c-word. It creates obstacles of doubt WITHIN YOU! The hardest person to defeat, is yourself.

One commonality across all doctrines and spiritual practices, is a reverence for words. A study conducted by Japanese scientist, Masaru Emoto, examined the effects of negative and positive words on pure water. The water in vials labeled 'I hate you' yielded gray misshapen clumps instead of beautiful crystalized ice. Guess what the result was from the vials labeled 'I love you'. It resulted in snow-flakes. This is one of many studies researching the energy of words. All platforms operate under the belief that 'Your words create your reality'.

What does that mean for you? How can you use this knowledge to your advantage? You now are aware of the power you have. Simply change what you are saying! Instead of saying, 'I am so out of shape' try 'I am getting healthier everyday' or 'Today I make healthier choices'. Are you familiar with the term 'self-fulfilling prophesy'?

A self-fulfilling prophecy refers to a belief or expectation that an individual hold about a future event that manifests because the individuals hold it. (Good Therapy, 2015)

We tend to believe what we say about selves, unconsciously we operate to make our statements truths.

Personally, for the past two years I've written a DAILY 'I am' list. My list reinforces the positive traits I have and speaks life into the traits I strive to have. I PROMISE YOU I embody these characteristics more each day.

The characteristics that I don't fully embody are like the pair of one-size-too-big school shoes we get every year. I have to grow into them.

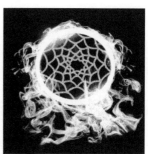

<u>Igniting Moment</u>

'The power of LIFE and DEATH lies in the tongue'

+Proverbs 18:21

BONUS

It might not be a surprise, but I have an intense love for the origin and meaning of words. Abracadabra is a Latin word that literally means, I create what I speak. Below list your magic words using 'I Am' statements. Do this daily and track your progress. Share your results with me at our Facebook page Ignited Ink 717.

My Magic Words

_____

_____

_____

_____

_____

_____

_____

_____

_____

_____

_____

_____

_____

_____

Can't???

I Can't do that!

I Can't do this!!!

Can't???

What's that??

Besides

Limitations

placed on us

By individuals who want to keep us small

Small enough to fit in their palms

To be folded eight times to fit in their WALLETS

I don't know about you

But I'm TIRED of being treated like POCKET-SIZED

origami

I'm convinced that my gray matter

Was formulated with the saaaammmmeee

Chemical composition as ALUMINUM

Because I think I CAN

Not a word that leaps forth of the diving boards of

man's lips

With the intentions to CANNON BALL

Into my thought STREAM can change my CURRENT

path

My convictions are too deep

To be slurred by words

So shallow

That they need life guard supervision and life jackets in

the kiddie pool

Do you feel the same?

Does your certainty illuminate BRIGHT enough

That a SHADOW of a doubt couldn't creep in

If not

Open yourself up to receive a couple of WATTS

YOUR dreams are NOT too big

YOUR dreams are NOT too big!

Your problem is your social circle

It has become a pretentious pajama party

And you are....

Pink-polished stained SLEEPING BAGS

And cotton candy scented BUNK BEDS

They are ALL just SLEEPING on you

Here's a shotgun ringing out in the library

Just in case you were sleeping on yourself

The seed wouldn't have been plated if your soil

couldn't produce it

So **believe!**

Until that seed cracks open and is rooted in your spirit

Water it daily with the words that come from the well

within

BELIEVE!!

Place solar panels on actions

And DOUBLE-TAP your PHOTOsynthesis

Until INSTAntly every GRAM of your heart is involved

We all know what happens to a dream that's deferred

Let's see what happens to a dream when it's nurtured

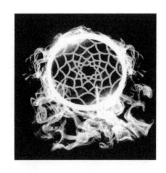

Igniting Moment

As you sail to your destiny, your faith will be tested. Currents of challenges will come and rock your boat. It is imperative to be anchored in your beliefs. Do not let the winds of doubt blow you off course.

As a proclaimed Christian in the 'woke' art community, I've received multitudinous questions about my belief. On some occasions questioned with earnest concern and on others bombarded by hostile interrogation. Both approaches taught me valuable lessons about myself. Personally, as an artist I figured my best response would be an artistic one. I wrote a poem titled, 'Holy Controversy', which explains why I believe in Jesus Christ. I address some of the rebuttals provided by my talented counterparts.

It is important to know WHY you believe, to ensure your faith is immovable. Especially, if what you believe drives you to succeed.

<u>Holy Controversy</u>

I'm not here to argue about His facial features

I'm not here to convert atheist into believers

I'm just trying to say

The way school need teachers

The way Kathy Lee needed Regis

That's the way I NEED Jesus

Jesus?!?!?!

How can you believe in Jesus?!

You all oil slick black

With midnight hidden in your melanin

Million man marching in your foot steps

Your fingertips still have nightmares

About 100% cotton

You eating that fruit of the gospel

And it's a 100% rotten

Swarming with time flies

Your history

You have 100% forgotten

I doubt your ancestor's hands were raised in praise

While on that slave ship

Willingly listening to the words of King James?

The sea, was an eye witness

seeing

script engraved in flesh

and preached in blood

on that slave ship

pieces of self

were executed

leaving voids the size of pot holes

your 'Holy Ghost' was birthed on that slave ship

take a guess

What was the name of the very first slave ship?

Jesus.

How can you believe in Jesus?!?!?!

Ok ok ok I know

You want to teach me a history lesson

Because you think

His-story has been used against me as a weapon

Hi-jacking my consciousness

And flying me into mindless obedience

But

One flick of this terror-wrist

Will show you why I believe

In Allah-the gospel about Jesus

You might say

'Ebony, you believe because that's all you've ever

heard'

I say

I believe because I've heard

Doctor's panicking

My mama soul pleading

My heart monitor singing in falsetto

And the kiss of death

Approaching holding mistletoes

But, Jesus

You might say

'Rose, you believe because that's all you've ever saw'

I say

It's because, I saw a shotgun house

Remolded by 17 gunshots

And the occupants sleep through the construction

I saw my mama…missing

I saw dried blood on the coffee table

I saw the signature of a nine-millimeter

A millimeter above where I was sleeping

I saw

Red and blue lights spray paint the sky

I thank God

I saw my mama

One hand as bloody as a battlefield

The other hand raised in liberty

Saying her pledge of allegiance

Thank you, Jesus

Now you want to know why I believe in Jesus?

I've seen cancer ridden bodies

Revived in the name of Jesus

I've seen AIDs run back to wherever it came from

In the name of Jesus

I've seen addictions broken

And people made whole

All in the name of Jesus

Now as for me

And all my poetry

Everything I write

And everything I recite

I will always end it

In the name of Jesus

"Everyone has been made for some particular work and the desire for that work has been put in every heart."
+ *Jalaluddin Rumi*

EXCELLENCE -VS- EXCUSES

The standard in which you operate influences everything and everyone around you. Do not allow yourself to be mediocre and others will follow suite. Are you familiar with the term 'Keeping up with the Jones''? It is an idiom utilized to depict living above your means to be seen as equal to those in higher tax brackets. When it comes to your circle, YOU ARE THE JONES'. You are the bar. If you want a better circle, elevate on all planes of existence. When the bar is raised, filtration will occur and toxic mediocrity will be eradicated.

'Aspire greatly; Anything less than a commitment to excellence becomes an acceptance of mediocrity.'

+Brian Tracy

In this game of life, you
only get one chance.
Luckily for you,
Excellence is the cheat code.
You decide.

FYI, you were not created to be mediocre being

your best self-unlocks the door to your best life.

FACT: Excellence and excuses cannot coexist. A

person of excellence is too determined to house

excuses. A person of excuses always has a reason why

they can't be excellent. I have deemed this type to be

a habitual presser of the 'but' button.

I was going to BUT

I tried to BUT

I want to BUT

you get the idea.

Do an honest assessment. Are you a person of excellence or are you always extending your hand to hit the BUT button?

When I was a child, I LOVED video games. I would play until my thumbs were sore. Are your thumbs sore from pressing the but button? Are you tired of playing...yourself?

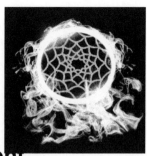

Igniting moment

'Excuses are tools of the incompetent used to build

bridges to nowhere and of nothingness, and those who

use them seldom specialize in anything else'

+Markeith Braden

EXPERT

Once you decide what you want to do, decide you are going to be the best you can be. (This is where the standard of excellence comes in). The true aim is to be the leader in your field. Imagine your name being associated with your expertise for generations to come.

Can you think of poetry without thinking about Maya Angelou or Shakespeare? Can you think of basketball without thinking of Michael Jordan or Kobe Bryant? If you are going to do it, you might as well give it your all. After all, what can it hurt?

You might ask, 'How do I become an expert'? My answer is to invest in your craft. If it will sharpen you, it is worth it. I'm not referring to just financial investments, the one thing more valuable than money is time. Do not spare any seconds when it comes to perfecting what you have in your hands. Take that extra hour to read the latest piece of literature that expounds on the trends. Do not look for shortcuts when it comes to spending millions of seconds researching, practicing, and perfecting. Practice is the key from going from good to great.

*WARNING Don't confuse reaching for excellence with perfectionism. If you wait to be perfect, your wait will never end. *

Michael Jordan and Kobe Bryant are idolized for their work effort. Former Lakers' player and head coach Bryon Scott, said he once found Bryant shooting in a dark gym TWO HOURS BEFORE PRACTICE. This is a resounding example of sacrifice and determination. What will you sacrifice to be your best?

Seriously!

What are willing to sacrifice to be your best?

Hint: Think about the activities you pour time into that doesn't help you get closer to your goal.

1)_____

2)_____

3)_____

4)_____

5)_____

6)_____

7)_____

I spend the most time

1)_____

2)_____

3)_____

4)_____

5)_____

6)_____

7)_____

Author of 'Outliers', Malcom Gladwell, states it takes roughly 10,000 hours of practice to achieve mastery in a field. That's dedication, commitment, motivation, AND tenacity. It is imperative that you build your dream on a **'No Matter What'** attitude.

What is the 'No Matter What' attitude?

When you operate with a 'No Matter What' mentality, you don't let anything stop you! Whatever you started will be completed with excellence! A mountain in your pathway doesn't stop the journey! You either find a way around it, through it, under it, or over it. I became privy of this phenomenon by way of Lisa Nichols, author of the best seller No Matter What. I eliminated excuses.

Ten thousand hours equates to roughly 20hours a week for 10 years. If you meet this idea with rejection, my question is.... How bad do you want it? If the concept of this level of work doesn't make you cringe,

you are ready.

Ready for **GREATNESS.**

<u>Ask Me</u>

The mirror has a glare that looks like 10,000 hours

Framed by exquisite expertise

These eyes the shade of scholar

These hands etched by work ethic

Even the marrow in my bones know

Every fact, statistic, and opinion

On this topic

I'm the top pick

Tick-tock, tock-tick

I'm the when and the how

Any questions, I'm the answer

'Be passion obsessed'

+Ebony Rose

MENTOR

Congratulations!!!

You have begun to shift your words into the realm of positivity. You stopped giving yourself the luxury of making excuses, and now you are ready to be all that you can be. What's next?

Would you voluntarily enter the depths of the jungle alone? Would you prefer a tour guide that has traveled the terrain daily to accompany you? I'm banking on this being a no brainer. However, for the adventure enthusiast, the answer is to have a tour guide. It only makes sense to follow someone who knows which plants are poisonous, what tree marks the lion's territory, and with which monkeys to not do business. A pivotal step in elevating your expertise is to get a mentor.

It's ideal to have a mentor that specializes in the field you are entering. It is possible to cross pollinate careers but make the seeds of knowledge you gather can be planted and harvested in your field.

When seeking a mentor be clear about your expectations. Taking the initiative to approach your mentor with an expectation, highlights the ambition and proactiveness in your character. Eagerness grabs the attention of leaders and puts everyone on notice that you are serious about elevating your career.

R-e-s-p-e-c-t is a requirement.

The task of yielding to/ learning from someone you don't respect/trust is more than difficult. Are you able to be clay in the potting hands of your mentor candidate? My mentors have aided in molding me professionally and spiritually. Mentors mold you, help you network, and call you out on your half-stepping.

61

MENTOR 101

Have a clear vision of the finish line, let your mentor know what you want to achieve, and if they can assist in meeting your goal. I suggest approaching your mentor-to-be with a resume highlighting what you have achieved in your field and any additional skills you possess or/and experience that are transferable in some way to your current position. Also, include a letter of intent that identifies areas you desire growth.

FOCUS

Prior to writing this book, I thought I had a working understanding of the word Focus. However, this process has taught me the true definition. I have eliminated all distractions. I am thankful for the self-awareness to know that drinking is a vice of mine. I haven't had a drink/a desire to drink since July 27, 2018. I formed a habit until drinking was my favorite past time, I noticed as I was passing time, time was passing me by. Some people can function while under the influence. Not I. I now have more, more time, more energy, and more money to invest in myself and my dreams.

What are you investing time in that you aren't getting a return on?

I declare on _____ __, 20__ I will no longer be distracted by _____.

When the going gets tough keep believing. If you see an obstacle as a reason to quit, you aren't ready to succeed.

'Obstacles only appear mountainous when you stand before them, they become miniscule molehills once you overcome them'

+Tiffany 'The Wordmatician' Scales

I'm not a runner by any means, but I love to see lean track stars leap over the hurdles. Their elongated legs stretching over the bar. It is a sight to see. When the hurdles are three feet apart, they keep leaping like the antelope. I've yet to see a race where a track star stopped to complain about the distance between hurdles. If the racer stopped, they would lose their momentum and their chance to win the race.

"Don't blow your chance to win, focusing on the reasons you'll lose'

+Ebony Rose

You get what you focus on. If you sow seeds of focus in knowing all the basketball stats, your harvest will resemble you spewing off statistics like a machine. Focus on what it looks like for you to win. Try your best to be as thorough as possible. Think about what a typical day in your winning life looks like. How are you dressed? What do you drive? What does your office look like? How is your mental health?   Tell us about it!

Today, my winning season looks like

_____

_____

_____

_____

_____

_____

_____

_____

_____

_____

_____

_____

_____

_____

_____

_____

_____

_____

_____

_____

Every winner knows how to turn a negative into a positive.

<u>Dope</u>

I knew I was going to be dope!

The moment I saw

My big cousin

Putting razor blade to crack

With laser precision

Turning our grandmother's kitchen table

Into BEDROCK

While

Thumbing through a thou

Like yabba-dabba-do

Right then and there

I inherited the recipe

To have them feening for these lines

Cook up a notebook quick, with the flick

of a bic pen

By the age of thirteen

I had more bars then the big pen

Now that's a sentence

Better yet a statement

Understand

Saying I'm blessed

Is an understatement

All my big cousins took a trip

to the big pen

Now that's a statement

No, I mean a sentence

(get it? prison sentence?)

My playground rumbled

With the appetite of hustlers

And gun play

Lacing Niks on powerlines

Kept them light on their feet

Ducking and dodging speeding bullets

Leaping over the hurdles of hunger pains

Itchy trigger fingers

With Stevie Wonder aim

My mama'll tell you

'A bullet don't have no name'

Somehow, I knew I was going to be the shooter

At the age of seven

I pulled that trigger with no hesitation

That day

And only that day!

Mama put a belt to my backside

I guess you can call that

A pistol whooping

Now, I'm loading these poems

With millimeter metaphors

And shotgun similes

Loading these lines, loading the lines

Armed and dangerous

With the truth

And my targets are your headshots

Which is to say, I want to blow your mind

Tickle your thoughts until your brain cells explode

Baby, I just want you open minded

Tonight, I want to welcome you to my gun range

Even if you don't catch a direct hit

I pray

You are tickled by the buck shots

BE YOUR OWN CHEERLEADER

Be positive.
Be, Be
Be, Be, Be positive.

At one point in time you will have to be your biggest cheerleader. There are pieces of the journey that will only be significant to you.   Your family and friends won't understand why you are full of glee when you get your DBA. Don't expect your every achievement and advancement to be applauded by others. Imagine

Something amazing happens getting you closer to your dreams then...

 BOOM the word is silent.

Even the faint chirps of the grasshoppers do not visit your celebratory moment.   Does that diminish the value?

Should you become discouraged?

What should you do?

Take your left hand, introduce it to your right hand AND

celebrate YOURSELF.

If this notion seems foreign or preposterous Take a

few things into consideration

1) Will this enhance the future of your career/ brand

or theirs?

It is rare that people celebrate something that

doesn't affect them or a cause they stand for....

CELEBRATE

2) Who did the work?

This occasion is the fruit of your labor, enjoy the

harvest ... CELEBRATE

Celebrate especially in your moments of failure. Cheer yourself on until your voice cracks and your throat bleeds. There will be times where you must fight...you! Combat your complacency, your comfort zone, your chronic procrastination, and catastrophic complaining. In the moments where the audience is booing with zeal, cheer louder.

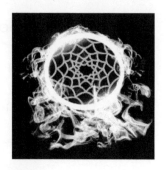

<u>IGNITING MOMENT</u>

The notion of self-love is drilled into our heads to the point, we ashamed if you don't. It is not easy to reveal the parts of you that make you cringe. There is a part of my life that's so dark, the brightest things were the shadows. My self-esteem was practically non-existent. I was even afraid to look in the mirror. I was LITERALLY AFRAID to see my reflection. In our selfie driven society, can you imagine that???

What do you love about you? For the next 30 days list ten things that you love about you! Share with us on our Facebook page and IgnitedInk717.com.

<u>Memoirs of the Mirror</u>

I'm the blackest seed my father could muster from his

deep soil

I'm the coal that blossomed in his soul

My toes to my nose sprung forth in the shadows as I was

wrapped in a midnight sky placenta inside the darkest

part of my mother's womb

could I be named anything other than... Ebony

My ink colored hands couldn't wait to grab this world in

my palms and leave my mark on it

caressing the crashing currents of deep blue oceans

'til the waves look like spilled ink running from the

aftermath of dropped vessels on ice white tile floors

finger painting continents 'til they look like 5 o'clock

shadows

'til the globe looks like the 1st day of creation

before God spoke "Let there be light"

Truth be told it was a battle embracing this dark sin

that shadows my bones

like a slave owner not wanting to be called ni**** lover

oh so long ago

It was suicide to let my dance blossom amongst the

sun's ultra violets, because then my black

would become blacker

A stain bleach couldn't get out

lifelong moon child, you wouldn't see me if the sun was

out

But why, when, how??? Did I want to run from my

mahogany melanin?

Answers march in, in the form of vintage voices that

echo in my ear

The bitter connotation that spilled from their lips

was like venom from a fang

when mentioning my daddy's oil dipped frame

Black,

black this,

black that,

you're so much like your daddy's black...

Ahhhhhhh, what a way to tarnish an innocent young

girl's heart, by poking at the tar of the man

who she resembles so vividly

you couldn't tell them apart

Searing flames loot in silence,

taking all I possessed

when the smoke clears

only damage remains

Third degree burns blister my heart

and scorch my soul

I want to scream I'm hurting!!!!!

but if you can't see it

I'm sure there's a wax build of nonchalant

dwelling in your ears as well

So, I will save my breath and use it as a cool breeze to

soothe my wounds

Some parts of me were burnt so badly,

now they are just ash blown in the wind

other parts of me are scarred, that I loved into beautiful

I can't remember

when I wrote my first love letter to the skin

I'm enveloped in

But I do know

it was filled with dark-and-lovely's

and sealed with blacker the berries

I look at this battered mirror and know I've made

progress

Because

I used to dodge my reflection like the plague,

the black plague

It was the boogeyman that made me hold my pillow

tight at night

It made my insides shiver like bones in a Chicago snow

storm

the question that haunted my waking dawns and quite

days,

what if the truth lied in what they said?

gasoline whispers met match stick tongues,

engulfed my haystack of self-esteem

But now everyday looking in the mirror

is physical and spiritual therapy for me

Gardening takes place in this mirror,

I use the faithful tool of God's truths to uproot the lies in

the garden of my heart

The wicked weeds taunted my orchids,

making them cry beauty,

'til they shrivel and die

despite what you may think God took his time and

designed you and I specifically

Before you left the womb

He put his stamp of approval on you

You are beautiful,

perfect because God doesn't make mistakes

wonderfully made

because everything God creates is good

next time you look in the mirror make sure you tell

yourself the truth

Courage

A pre-requisite for success is courage. My favorite definition of courage is not the absence of fear but acting in the face of fear. A fear most people can relate to, is the fear of the dark. You can't see what is ahead. You have no idea what is lurking around you. What if the next step leads to a bottomless pit? If the fear of the unknown halts your progress the journey of discovery will never begin. Fear is birthed out of our insecurities. If the dark is the fear, what is the light? What will make you keep going? What flicks the light switch of courage?

Fear is a device designed to derail you. The threat of fear can steer you from your path. Many people never start the journey because they are stuck writing the what if list.

What if this happens?

What if that happens?

What if

What if

What if

Even if your worst fear comes true, you will survive
.... Thrive.

Have the courage to believe!

<u>WORK</u>

There isn't a way around this. Work cannot be avoided. The least of success requires work. Can you think of anything great that was achieved that didn't require great work ethic? Here are a few great labors of time that have stood the test of time

- 16th Chapel took four years to complete- since 1483
- Mount Rushmore took 14 years to complete – since 1941
- The Great Wall of China took 20 years to complete – 221 BC
- Rome- approximately 1,009,491 days

You my dear are a great labor of time. Don't rush your greatness. However, sow into your greatness every day. Don't let how much time it takes stop you from getting started.

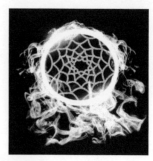

IGNITING MOMENT

'Your DNA doesn't determine your destiny'
+Ebony Rose

BONUS

Addiction is a beast that the owner doesn't want to tame. The addict is too entertained by the beast's wild and unpredictable behavior. My family lineage is a zoo. According to Addictions and Recovery, fifty percent of addiction is due to a genetic predisposition. The moment I was conceived I was already more likely than most to be an addict. I've experienced the unrelentless hold alcohol can have even after watching its grip choke the ambition and life out of those around me. I thank God I was able to slip between its fingers. Are you an addict? Does your family suffer from this plague?

<u>Family Plot</u>

Hello, Grim reaper, I see you here often

slaughtering dreams by the masses before they are

conceived

you even put abortions in the coffin

Viciously performing vasectomies on vulnerable victims

If they even think about a seed

When wounded minds seek healing, you show up

coughing

Infecting their white blood cells of optimism

I see you plotting

I'm sure your address book has entries from A to Z

And your appointment book has your handwriting on

every line

Next to every day and every time

With the millions of families at existing at this time

Why do you make yourself at home with mine?

Maybe you receive some sick pleasure poising their

minds

As they poison themselves to endure the torture with

anything

In the gutter they can find

To be content within the wretched walls that have

them confined

You spit acid of poverty, and despair in their eyes

so now are they not only in the dark, you also have
them blind

are you not entertained?!

Watching them in slow-mo as they loosen their grips
and let hope go

saying hello to the X-Os and dro smoke believing that
crack is a loving fellow

believing old English bottles more than the old English in
the bible

are you not entertained?!

You robbed them of the essence of their youthful years

Stole that which can't be returned

Placed them in an asylum of addition

Restrained their growth, you put a strait jacket on time

Decades later, replaying the mistakes you caused

them to make

Now, failure is the only word they hear

When the voice of their reflection speaks

it echoes from the pit of hollowness you dug in their

souls

which has been ripped and torn into a black hole

suspended in this space between heaven and hell in

midair,

gluttonous in its desires, it never gets full

Hello, monkey on the back

You have eaten here for generations

Swallowing us whole

digesting us in your stomach without table manners or

hesitation

but not before you let us cook up pro-creation

sometimes you were present for the preparation

seeing your next meal go from thought to

manifestation

dope is in the room, while the baby's in the womb

that was your appetizer you were tasting at the tomb

what you could do next to devour our flesh

feast on our futures dine on our destinies and pick the

bones of our purpose clean

and make our bloodline worthless

I know my blood line is worth it, that's why I wrote this

Our blood line is corrupted by one of those

generational curses

And we continue to pay homage in blood…what a

vicious cycle

Hemorrhaging in the mud and still not enough

I'm convinced my family tree is rooted in the decaying

soil of a grave

That goes back further than many fathers

I don't know my grandfather so I had to look harder

At the freeloading demons our DNA harbors

To read the name on the tombstone

Home of the first wicked seed

That only will produce rotting fruit with noose dangling

from the tree

Making us submitting slaves to the master of addiction

Readily obeying his every command, stroking his ego

Don't want to rub him the wrong way or cause any

friction

You were convinced love would flow effortlessly

through that crack pipe

But the waves of depression crashed on you last night

The enemy is a hustler slanging lies and false hope

Disguised as liquor, pills, green and dope

He can't hang ya but he can provide the rope

And deceive you by telling you the sweetest fruit is at

the top of this tree

So you get high, high, high

Not knowing the branches stretch far past the stars and

the sky

Its only so high our human lungs will allow us travel

Before we crash.

ABOUT THE AUTHOR

Childhood surroundings were more fertilizer than fertile. Ebony Rose. She is proof that a concrete slab doesn't beat persistence. It couldn't stop a determined seed from reaching through its cracks and blossoming. Ebony Rose. She's always had a passion for writing whether it was short stories, rap songs, or research papers. It was destiny fueled by purpose when God revealed to her that she was designed to be a poet. Now she travels across state lines sharing her gift to encourage and enlighten others. Ebony Rose. She's petaled poems across stages in her city of Houston bestowing knowledge, encouragement, and the gospel upon the masses. Ebony Rose has opened for 90's superstar MC Yoyo, was a featured artist for Super Bowl LI live, showcased at Houston Public Library's tribute to Prince, placed in the top five at the 2017 National Poetry Slam, starred in the thrilling stage play 'Bandaged Wounds', hosted her own radio show 'The Artist's Corner', holds the position as Creative Director for Sol-Poetry, and so much more. CEO of Ignited Ink 717 and Partner of The Arts Advocate, she has a podcast, Long Live The Arts, a book, Spark A Dream and album, Late Bloomer coming soon. She continues to allow her gift to make room for her. Ebony Rose.